JMn

‖‖‖ ‖‖‖‖‖ ‖‖ ‖ ‖‖‖ ‖‖‖‖‖‖‖‖‖‖‖‖ ‖‖‖

W9-AXZ-059

THURGOOD MARSHALL

The African-American Biographies Series

MARIAN ANDERSON
Singer and Humanitarian
0-7660-1211-5

MAYA ANGELOU
More Than a Poet
0-89490-684-4

LOUIS ARMSTRONG
King of Jazz
0-89490-997-5

ARTHUR ASHE
Breaking the Color Barrier
in Tennis
0-89490-689-5

BENJAMIN BANNEKER
Astronomer and Mathematician
0-7660-1208-5

JULIAN BOND
Civil Rights Activist
and Chairman of the NAACP
0-7660-1549-1

RALPH BUNCHE
Winner of the Nobel Peace Prize
0-7660-1203-4

**GEORGE WASHINGTON
CARVER**
Scientist and Inventor
0-7660-1770-2

BESSIE COLEMAN
First Black Woman Pilot
0-7660-1545-9

FREDERICK DOUGLASS
Speaking Out Against Slavery
0-7660-1773-7

W. E. B. DU BOIS
Champion of Civil Rights
0-7660-1209-3

**PAUL LAURENCE
DUNBAR**
Portrait of a Poet
0-7660-1350-2

DUKE ELLINGTON
Giant of Jazz
0-89490-691-7

ARETHA FRANKLIN
Motown Superstar
0-89490-686-0

NIKKI GIOVANNI
Poet of the People
0-7660-1238-7

WHOOPI GOLDBERG
Comedian and Movie Star
0-7660-1205-0

FANNIE LOU HAMER
Fighting for the Right to Vote
0-7660-1772-9

LORRAINE HANSBERRY
Playwright and Voice of Justice
0-89490-945-2

MATTHEW HENSON
Co-Discoverer of the North Pole
0-7660-1546-7

LANGSTON HUGHES
Poet of the Harlem Renaissance
0-89490-815-4

ZORA NEALE HURSTON
Southern Storyteller
0-89490-685-2

JESSE JACKSON
Civil Rights Activist
0-7660-1390-1

QUINCY JONES
Musician, Composer, Producer
0-89490-814-6

BARBARA JORDAN
Congresswoman, Lawyer,
Educator
0-89490-692-5

CORETTA SCOTT KING
Striving for Civil Rights
0-89490-811-1

**MARTIN LUTHER
KING, JR.**
Leader for Civil Rights
0-89490-687-9

JOHN LEWIS
From Freedom Rider to Congressman
0-7660-1768-0

THURGOOD MARSHALL
Civil Rights Attorney and
Supreme Court Justice
0-7660-1547-5

KWEISI MFUME
Congressman and NAACP Leader
0-7660-1237-9

TONI MORRISON
Nobel Prize-Winning Author
0-89490-688-7

WALTER DEAN MYERS
Writer for Real Teens
0-7660-1206-9

JESSE OWENS
Track and Field Legend
0-89490-812-X

COLIN POWELL
Soldier and Patriot
0-89490-810-3

A. PHILIP RANDOLPH
Union Leader
and Civil Rights Crusader
0-7660-1544-0

PAUL ROBESON
Actor, Singer, Political Activist
0-89490-944-4

JACKIE ROBINSON
Baseball's Civil Rights Legend
0-89490-690-9

BETTY SHABAZZ
Sharing the Vision
of Malcolm X
0-7660-1210-7

HARRIET TUBMAN
Moses of the Underground Railroad
0-7660-1548-3

MADAM C. J. WALKER
Self-Made Businesswoman
0-7660-1204-2

IDA B. WELLS-BARNETT
Crusader Against Lynching
0-89490-947-9

OPRAH WINFREY
Talk Show Legend
0-7660-1207-7

CARTER G. WOODSON
Father of African-American History
0-89490-946-0

RICHARD WRIGHT
Author of *Native Son* and *Black Boy*
0-7660-1769-9

—African-American Biographies—

THURGOOD MARSHALL

Civil Rights Attorney and Supreme Court Justice

Series Consultant:
Dr. Russell L. Adams, Chairman
Department of Afro-American Studies, Howard University

Mark Rowh

Enslow Publishers, Inc.

40 Industrial Road   PO Box 38
Box 398   Aldershot
Berkeley Heights, NJ 07922   Hants GU12 6BP
USA   UK

http://www.enslow.com

Library of Congress Cataloging-in-Publication Data

Rowh, Mark.
    Thurgood Marshall : civil rights attorney and Supreme Court justice / Mark Rowh.
        p. cm. — (African-American biographies)
    Includes bibliographical references and index.
    Summary: Traces the life, accomplishments, and legacy of the civil rights attorney who became a prominent Supreme Court Justice.
    ISBN 0-7660-1547-5
    1. Marshall, Thurgood, 1908–1993—Juvenile literature. 2. United States. Supreme Court—Biography—Juvenile literature. 3. Judges—United States—Biography—Juvenile literature. [1. Marshall, Thurgood, 1908–1993. 2. Lawyers. 3. Judges. 4. African Americans—Biography.]
I. Title. II. Series.
    KF8745.M34 R69 2001
    347.73'2634—dc21

                             2001003141

Printed in the United States of America

10 9 8 7 6 5 4 3 2 1

To Our Readers:
We have done our best to make sure all Internet Addresses in this book were active and appropriate when we went to press. However, the author and the publisher have no control over and assume no liability for the material available on those Internet sites or on other Web sites they may link to. Any comments or suggestions can be sent by e-mail to comments@enslow.com or to the address on the back cover.

Every effort has been made to locate all copyright holders of material used in this book. If any errors or omissions have occurred, corrections will be made in future editions of this book.

Illustration Credits: Art by Simmie L. Knox, Collection of the Supreme Court of the United States, p. 95; Collection of the Supreme Court of the United States, pp. 9, 13, 19, 26; Courtesy of the Maryland State Archives Special Collections, p. 98; Library of Congress, pp. 28, 30, 36, 66, 75; National Archives, pp. 41, 53, 58, 71; Photo by Deborah L. Rhode, Collection of the Supreme Court of the United States, p. 83; Photo by Hessler-Studios (1967–1970), Collection of the Supreme Court of the United States, p. 78; Photo by Robert S. Oaks, Collection of the Supreme Court of the United States, p. 86; Photo by Will Counts, pp. 51, 55.

Cover Illustration: Collection of the Supreme Court of the United States.

CONTENTS

Acknowledgments

The author would like to thank all those who made the development of this manuscript possible, including the following:

Dr. Jerold Dugger
Franz Jantzen
National Archives and Records Administration
Naydine Shenk
The Supreme Court of the United States
West Virginia State College

1

LAWYER FOR THE PEOPLE

That day in March 1946 seemed like a typical one at the United States Supreme Court. Seated in their black robes were nine dignified justices. All were men. All were white. As usual, the case before them dealt with a decision that had been made at a lower-level court. The Supreme Court was about to take another look at the ruling.

A young African-American man stepped forward. Tall and well-spoken, the attorney stood out. African-American lawyers were not a common sight, especially in the nation's highest court. Even so, the justices had seen this man before. He had already presented three cases before them. Attorney Thurgood Marshall worked for a group known as the National Association for the Advancement of Colored People (NAACP).

In this case, he represented a black woman named Irene Morgan. The Baltimore resident had been traveling on a Greyhound bus in Virginia when the driver asked her to move to the back to make room for some white passengers. In the South at that time, laws kept the races separate and gave better treatment to white people.

But Morgan refused to give up her seat. As a result, she was arrested. It was a humiliating experience. Morgan did not think it was right, but she was found guilty of breaking the law and forced to pay a fine.

Morgan appealed the case, but the appeal was denied. So she took it to the Supreme Court of Virginia with the assistance of Spottswood Robinson, a Howard University law professor. Once again, judges affirmed the original guilty verdict. Then Robinson, with the help of Marshall and the NAACP, appealed to the United States Supreme Court.[1]

The justices knew all this background, but they needed to hear more. So Marshall explained just why the verdict was wrong. He presented solid, well-researched arguments, citing earlier laws and court rulings going back to the 1870s. He said that when people traveled from one state to another, state laws supporting segregation no longer applied. This was

As a lawyer for the NAACP, Thurgood Marshall fought against racial discrimination.

true, he argued, because the right to conduct interstate commerce, which included travel, was a basic right protected by the Constitution.

Then he made a connection with more recent history. He referred to World War II, which had ended less than a year before. In that war, he noted, Americans had fought together against the Nazis, whom many considered the ultimate racists. It did not make sense now to use racist practices to restrict the rights of people to travel within the United States.[2]

Those familiar with the case praised Marshall for doing a great job. His arguments were sound. They appealed not just to obscure legal concepts but to basic principles of the Constitution. Later, a distinguished judge called the arguments written by Marshall and the NAACP legal team "a marvel of advocacy."[3] In addition, Marshall had a special flair for communicating his ideas in a convincing way. He was becoming something of a star in the legal world.

Morgan, Marshall, and the others involved in the case had to wait for months as the justices considered the matter. It was worth the wait. When the Court finally announced its verdict, it found in favor of Irene Morgan. By a 7 to 1 vote, the justices held that it was wrong to make her give up her seat. Because she was traveling from one state to another, the principles of interstate commerce applied. This meant that it was unfair for one state's laws (in this case Virginia's segregation laws) to limit her rights.[4]

The ruling did not mean that segregation within states was stopped. That battle remained to be fought. Yet the decision, though a small one, was an important victory for the NAACP and for African Americans everywhere.

It was also a triumph for Marshall personally. This young lawyer clearly knew what he was doing. He was smart. He was aggressive. And he was dedicated to fighting against racial discrimination.

Those who wanted to continue long-standing racist practices, in which African Americans were denied the rights of other citizens, had better look out. Thurgood Marshall was fighting for change—and if his performance so far was any indication, the future looked bright.

2

EARLY DAYS

hurgood Marshall was born on July 2, 1908, in Baltimore, Maryland. His parents, William and Norma Arica Marshall, were descended from African slaves and white residents of Virginia and Maryland. Thurgood's brother, William Aubrey, was three years old.

Family members enjoyed telling the story of their most notorious ancestor. A native of the Congo, in Africa, he was captured by a big-game hunter and taken to America to be a slave. Later, according to family legend, the boy caused so much trouble that his master set him free just to be rid of him.[1]

Thurgood, age one.

Thurgood Marshall was named after his great-grandfather Thoroughgood. When he learned to write, the younger Thoroughgood grew tired of spelling out such a long name. So in elementary school he shortened his name to Thurgood.[2]

In 1910, the Marshall family moved to Harlem, a neighborhood in New York City. Thurgood's aunt Denmedia, called Medi by her nephews, had urged the family to move there so William Marshall could get a job on the New York Central Railroad. She said she would help care for Thurgood and his brother if they lived nearby.[3]

Living in New York City was exciting for Thurgood and his family. Even though Baltimore was also a major city, New York offered new sights and sounds. One difference was that throngs of people had come from elsewhere to live in New York. Although most immigrants in Baltimore had come from Europe, New York was more diverse. The population included many black immigrants from Africa, the Caribbean, and the American South.[4]

When Thurgood was six, his grandmother broke her leg, and the family moved back to Baltimore to care for her. His mother took a job as a teacher, and his father worked as a waiter. The Marshalls lived comfortably, and the family dinner table rang with lively conversation. Thurgood's parents enjoyed talking about current events, and Mr. Marshall encouraged his sons to express their opinions. The family's friendly "arguments" played a key role in developing Thurgood's communication skills.[5]

The Marshall house was located in a respectable African-American neighborhood in a middle-class part of the city called Druid Hill. Nearby neighborhoods were more run-down. Some of the children were considered tough kids, but Thurgood was not afraid of them. An aunt said, "He wasn't any Mama-dress-me-and-send-me-to-Sunday-school sort of boy. He was always a smart, alert little fella, full of life and laughter."[6]

Whether indoors or outside, young Thurgood Marshall was not the quiet type. In addition to being talkative, he was full of energy. In school he sometimes got into trouble. At his grade school, unruly students were often sent to the basement as punishment. Thurgood was banished this way a number of times. Part of the punishment was to memorize sections of the U.S. Constitution. As a result, Thurgood became very familiar with the Constitution—the most important document defining the principles of the American way of life. "Before I left that school, I knew the whole thing by heart," he later claimed.[7]

At school and at home, Thurgood Marshall's world differed greatly from ours today. There was no television. Some people had automobiles, but most could not afford them. Women were not allowed to vote until 1920. Many jobs and careers were for men only.

Socially and legally, minority groups did not share the same rights and opportunities as white Americans. Almost all black Americans were the descendants of people stolen from their homelands to serve as slaves in the United States. Even though slavery had been abolished in the 1860s, the prejudices of the past still held strong.

For the most part people lived, worshiped, and traveled only with others of their own race. Most white Americans believed that black Americans were inferior and did not deserve equal treatment. The law was on their side: Many states had laws, known as "Jim Crow" laws, that made segregation legal.

In many areas of the nation, African Americans were not allowed to live in the same neighborhoods as white citizens or attend the same schools. In the southern part of the country, they could not eat in the same restaurants or attend many of the same entertainment or sporting events. When they were allowed to attend, they had to sit in separate sections, such as the back of a bus and the balcony of a movie theater.

Thurgood Marshall's home in West Baltimore was in a racially mixed neighborhood, with whites and blacks, Christians and Jews.[8] Although Thurgood had a happy childhood, racial discrimination had a very real impact on his life. His father's job choices were limited and his salary was lower than that of most white workers. The same held true for his mother. Although she was a qualified teacher, she earned less money than the white teachers.

As a very young child, Thurgood was unaware of racial problems. Then, at age seven, he was surprised when a playmate used a racial slur. When Thurgood asked his parents what it meant, they used the incident to talk about racial discrimination. His father also said that if anyone called him a racist name, "You not only got my permission to fight him—you got my orders to fight him."[9]

Marshall's family was neither poor nor rich. They lived comfortably, but there was never a lot of extra money to go around. As a boy, Thurgood worked at a number of different jobs. He was only seven when he took his first job as an errand boy for a grocery store.[10] Over the years, he worked at a variety of other jobs, including being a delivery boy and carrying bags for guests at a hotel.

Always a big joker, Marshall once said, "There's no call for a man to ever lift anything much heavier than a poker chip."[11] But the truth was that he was a hard worker and did whatever a job required.

As a teenager, Marshall worked part-time at a hat company. Once, in a hurry to deliver some hats, he rushed onto a streetcar. A stranger on the streetcar insulted Marshall with a racist name and ordered him to stay out of the way of white people. Marshall immediately "tore into" the man, as he described the incident later, and ended up getting arrested for fighting. His boss at the hat company came to the police station to get him out.[12]

Although such incidents opened his eyes to the problems of segregation, Marshall's youth was generally happy. He liked sports but was not a talented athlete. He later joked that he gave up playing baseball when two sandlot teams threatened to go on strike if either team had to take him as a player. Instead of playing sports, Marshall got more pleasure out of watching them. He especially liked baseball and football.

From an early age, Thurgood loved to argue. If he was told the sky is blue, he might disagree, saying that it just looked that way. He loved to talk about all kinds of things. He was quick to ask just what his friends or relatives thought about any issue, and he was even quicker to voice his own opinion.

Sometimes Thurgood attended court with his father. William Marshall was intrigued by trials and by the law in general. He had not had the opportunity to go to college, but he wanted to learn about public affairs. Often he attended trials just because he was interested. When Thurgood went along, he also found the law fascinating.

Marshall's father loved to argue about current

From an early age, Thurgood liked to argue. Sometimes this got him into trouble at school.

events and enjoyed involving his sons in family debates. He taught them to speak their minds and, even more important, to back up what they said with facts. Thurgood Marshall later said that even though his father never directly urged him to become an attorney, "he turned me into one. He did it by teaching me to argue, by challenging my logic on every point, by making me prove every statement I made."[13]

Thurgood too often saw the ugliness of racial discrimination, but he did not personally face the violence that plagued African Americans in some other parts of the United States. In 1919 alone, at least twenty-five race riots occurred in other states, and more than one hundred African Americans were murdered.[14] Many of the killings were lynchings, in which gangs of white men hanged blacks in a frenzy of mob hatred.

These racial problems were not a part of Marshall's young life. At the age of sixteen, when he graduated from high school, he was not overly concerned about civil rights. Instead, he was a typical teenager focused on enjoying life and planning for college.

3

COLLEGE AND BEYOND

In September 1925, Marshall began studying at Lincoln University in Oxford, Pennsylvania. The college was not too far from Baltimore, and it admitted African Americans. All the students were members of minority groups, but most of the professors were white.[1] This was not unusual at the time for schools known as Negro institutions.

During the 1920s, Lincoln University's reputation was on the upswing; it was known informally as "the black Princeton." Many of the school's faculty were

Princeton University graduates, and Lincoln adopted the same school colors as Princeton.[2]

In the early part of his college career, Marshall was not very serious about studying. He was more interested in having a good time: staying up late, playing cards, and hanging out with friends. Like the other freshmen, he wore short pants, high socks held up with garters, and a blue hat called a beanie. It was all part of being a first-year student at Lincoln in the 1920s.[3]

Marshall was not sure what he wanted to study. His mother had encouraged him to become a dentist, but he did not like the science courses that profession required. Instead, he decided to focus on the liberal arts.

As in high school, Marshall was a lively sort who sometimes got into trouble. During his sophomore year, he became involved in hazing, a practice of picking on new students or those who wanted to join fraternities and other organized groups. Hazing at colleges and universities usually involved harmless pranks, but sometimes it got out of hand and resulted in injuries or deaths. Hazing often brought severe punishments.

Marshall and some fellow students pulled stunts such as paddling freshmen and shaving their heads. When they were caught, Marshall and his friends were expelled. They had to leave school for a while, but after apologizing for their behavior, they were readmitted.

One of Marshall's favorite activities was debating. He enjoyed friendly arguments with other students and was a natural for the debate team. He joined the team as a freshman and later became one of its outstanding members. A highlight came when the debate team traveled to Boston and competed against teams from some of the greatest schools in the world, including Harvard University and Great Britain's Cambridge University.[4]

Marshall was full of energy and always on the go. Once, when running to catch a ride in a pickup truck, he fell and was badly injured. By the time he recovered, he was a semester behind his classmates. When he returned to college, he was more serious about his studies. "I got the horsin' around out of my system," he said later.[5]

During this time he read widely and became especially interested in works by African-American authors. This included works by writer and civil rights leader W. E. B. Du Bois, as well as *The Negro in Our History*, by Carter G. Woodson, and *The American Negro*, by Jerome Dowd.[6]

Marshall also began dating an outgoing young woman from Philadelphia. Vivian Burey was a student at the University of Pennsylvania. Thurgood and Buster, as he called her, fell in love and decided to get married. Their wedding took place in 1929 at the First African Baptist Church in Philadelphia. After the wedding, Buster moved to Baltimore to live with Marshall's parents while Marshall returned to Lincoln to finish his degree.[7]

That October, the country experienced a dramatic change. The stock market crashed when the value of stocks dropped quickly. Many people lost all their money. The next ten years were known as the Great Depression. Banks, factories, and stores went out of business, and thousands of Americans lost their jobs. It was a time of terrible poverty.

Marshall graduated from college with honors in January 1930. It was quite an accomplishment for someone who had not taken school very seriously at first. But finding a job during the depression was not easy. For a while Marshall worked as an insurance agent, but he hated the job. He found it boring. He went back to being a waiter, which he had done during summer breaks from college. At the same time, he made plans for his career: He would go to law school.

Marshall wanted to go to the University of Maryland Law School, near his home. It had a good reputation and the tuition was affordable. But no African Americans had been admitted to the law school for more than thirty years. Marshall decided there was no point in even applying.[8]

Instead Marshall applied to the law school at Howard University. It was not far away, in Washington, D.C., and the student body was African American. But coming up with the money for tuition was a challenge for Marshall. Although he had saved as much as he could, it was not enough. His mother pawned her wedding ring and her engagement ring to come up with the rest of the money.[9] His wife worked too, contributing what she could to the family income.

Marshall knew that becoming an attorney would not be easy, but the work appealed to him. Out of 160,000 attorneys practicing at the time, only about 1,000—far less than one percent—were African American.[10] Marshall was willing to work hard to become one of them.

Law school was a three-year program. In his studies to become a lawyer, Marshall's most unforgettable professor was Charles Hamilton Houston. This brilliant scholar was one of the first people to inspire Marshall to fight for civil rights. He was one of the most influential people in Marshall's life.

Not only was Houston a talented scholar, he was also a demanding teacher who insisted that his students work extremely hard. Marshall said that Houston was so tough that many students called him "Iron Pants" and "Cement Drawers" and other names. But Marshall also developed great respect for Houston and grew to understand how much he was learning from this strict professor."[11]

Charles Houston was a leading civil rights activist. A highly accomplished lawyer, he handled a number

When Marshall started college, he was still full of youthful pranks. By the time he entered law school, though, he had become a serious and successful student. In this photo he is in the second row, fifth from left.

of cases for African Americans. Many of these groundbreaking efforts set the stage for later legal struggles for equal rights.

Inspired by Houston and other professors, Marshall worked harder than ever before. "I heard lawbooks were to dig in," he later said. "So I dug way deep."[12] His efforts paid off. At the end of his three years of law school, Marshall ranked at the head of his class.[13]

Marshall graduated from Howard University Law School in 1933. He took the bar exam required to practice law in Maryland and passed on the first attempt. At last he was ready to start his career. Instead of going to work for someone else's firm, he decided to open his own law practice in Baltimore.

This was a very difficult time to make a living, in law as in many other fields. The entire United States was suffering from the hard times of the Great Depression. Economic conditions were especially difficult for African Americans. Many had low-paying jobs or relied on welfare—money from the government.

The first year was a tough one. Marshall handled small cases such as disputes between tenants and landlords, but they did not pay much. His main focus was not on making money. Sometimes he represented people who could not pay him at all. During the first year, his practice actually lost about $1,000.[14] To earn extra money, he worked part-time as a file clerk at a health clinic, and his wife worked as a sales clerk.

Marshall became increasingly interested in the prospect of using the legal system to advance the goals of the National Association for the Advancement of Colored People (NAACP). This organization, formed by white and black civil rights activists in 1909, had emerged as the major group dedicated to equal rights for African Americans.

The NAACP members were from all over the United States. Being a national association gave the NAACP strength; it had more clout than state or regional

Marshall, left, opened his first law practice in Baltimore.

groups. The NAACP was ready to get involved anywhere people asked for assistance, even in states with Jim Crow laws or other statutes that limited civil rights.

Marshall believed in the importance of the law in maintaining a peaceful society. He also knew that some laws were unfair—but that laws could be changed. As an attorney, Marshall wanted to work within the legal system to improve the lives of African Americans. Almost from the start of his law practice, Marshall considered suing the University of Maryland over its admission practices. It was wrong that he and other African Americans could not attend school there. One of Marshall's goals was eventually to challenge the university in court and force it to change its discriminatory practices.

Most of Marshall's early legal work was done in Baltimore, but he also learned more about the discrimination facing African Americans in other parts of the United States. Especially important was a car trip Marshall took with Charles Houston through several southern states. This was the first time Marshall had ever traveled farther south than the Washington, D.C., area. It was an eye-opening trip. Marshall was shocked by the poverty and racism he encountered. He learned that in the South, segregation was practiced more widely and openly than in the North.

A few of Marshall's cases began to bring him recognition. In 1934 he felt ready to challenge the

Marshall, left, and NAACP attorney Charles Houston, right, sued the University of Maryland's law school for refusing to admit Donald Gaines Murray, center.

University of Maryland. Donald Murray, an African-American college graduate, was rejected by Maryland's law school because of his race. Marshall and Charles Houston went to the city court and asked the judge to consider the case. After reviewing the facts, the judge made a groundbreaking decision: The law school would have to admit Donald Murray after all.

This was Marshall's first civil rights victory. It was not just a personal triumph; it was also an important step forward for African Americans.

4

CIVIL RIGHTS ADVOCATE

In 1936, Marshall learned of an opening for a professor at the Howard University Law School. He applied for the position, thinking that teaching law would be an interesting job with a dependable salary.

But Marshall's former law professor Charles Houston had other ideas in mind. He had left Howard University and was working as special legal counsel for the NAACP. Houston wanted Marshall to join him, and he persuaded NAACP officials to allow him to offer Marshall a job.

It did not take Marshall long to decide. After all, he

was a fighter. He believed that to effect change, you have to take action. It is not enough just to complain. Marshall also wanted people who needed legal help to get it, even if they could not afford to pay much. He knew there was a great deal of work to be done for African Americans.

Marshall took the job, and he and his wife relocated to New York City. They moved to Harlem, home to a large population of African Americans. Poets, novelists, artists, musicians, and others who lived there made Harlem a focus of African-American art and culture, and it was an exciting place to live. The Marshalls enjoyed their new home. They often visited popular nightspots to hear jazz played by stars such as Duke Ellington, who had been a classmate of Marshall's at Lincoln University.

But Marshall's main focus was on his work. The challenge was huge. A major barrier to civil rights for African Americans was a Supreme Court decision made in 1896, long before Marshall was born. It was still in effect. In this important case, known as *Plessy* v. *Ferguson*, the Supreme Court had made its famous "separate but equal" ruling. The justices said that black Americans and white Americans were entitled to separate but equal rights in such areas as education and use of public facilities. This sounded fair, for the ruling seemed to promote equality. But it meant that it was legal in the United States to segregate people based on race. And in reality, the facilities for blacks were far from equal to the facilities for whites.

The interpretation of the law to promote segregation, plus various state laws and practices followed by businesses and institutions, were what the NAACP was fighting to change.

The job kept Marshall busy. Along with his New York operations, he kept an office in Baltimore at his mother's home so he could finish the work he had started with clients there. "Between 1936 and 1938, I commuted practically between Baltimore and New York, and there was considerable practice in that period," he said later.[1]

One of the first problems Marshall tackled was equal pay for equal work. Black Americans' salaries were often much lower than those of white Americans who performed the same jobs. This was true of schoolteachers in Maryland, including Marshall's own mother. Black teachers earned as much as 40 percent less than white teachers, even when they had the same qualifications.[2]

Marshall looked for an opportunity to challenge this practice in court. He took on two cases in Maryland. The first settled out of court when Montgomery County agreed to equalize pay between teachers of both races. The second was a clear-cut victory in which Marshall's impressive courtroom skills played a key role in winning the case. After ruling that

Maryland's Anne Arundel County schools unfairly discriminated against African-American teachers, the judge ordered that salaries be equalized. Not only did the case help teachers in that county, but it led to a law equalizing salaries for all teachers in Maryland.[3]

Marshall then pursued similar cases in other states, and he won most of them. Before long, teachers around the country were earning equal pay regardless of race. Marshall was doing excellent work. When Charles Houston decided in 1938 to give up the demanding job of chief legal officer for the NAACP, his obvious replacement was Thurgood Marshall. Houston nominated him, and Marshall agreed to take the job.

The NAACP was fortunate at times to receive the backing of other groups that promoted human rights or civil rights. These included the American Civil Liberties Union (ACLU), the American Federation of Labor, and the Society of Friends (Quakers).[4] But despite their support, which sometimes included financial backing, lack of funding was often a problem.

One of Marshall's earliest accomplishments at the NAACP was to set up a new way for people to donate money to the organization. He created a new branch, the NAACP Defense and Educational Fund, Inc. It had tax-exempt status, which encouraged donations because people were more likely to give if doing so would help to lower their income taxes.[5]

At the same time, Marshall realized that the success

of legal actions did not depend solely on the support of well-meaning donors. It also rested on the bravery of men and women who were willing to step forward to challenge segregation. This was not easy in the hostile environments of many southern states.

Fighting for progress meant sticking one's neck out. In the South, African-American attorneys and others who spoke out against injustice took great risks. If they filed a lawsuit or testified in court about segregation, they were labeled troublemakers. They might be fired from their jobs, physically attacked, or otherwise mistreated. And long after an out-of-town lawyer had left to pursue other cases, the African Americans he had represented still faced the dangerous resentment of local bigots.[6]

Marshall was willing to take risks. He could not just sit in New York and provide legal advice by mail or telephone. Some of his work could be accomplished in New York, but it was increasingly clear that travel was a key part of his job. He would go to the southern cities where his legal cases could make a difference.

Traveling into the Deep South to represent African Americans in court, Marshall did more than provide legal assistance. He also served as an example—to both blacks and whites—that a black American professional was just as competent as a white. This is obvious today, but it was not the case years ago. Many people

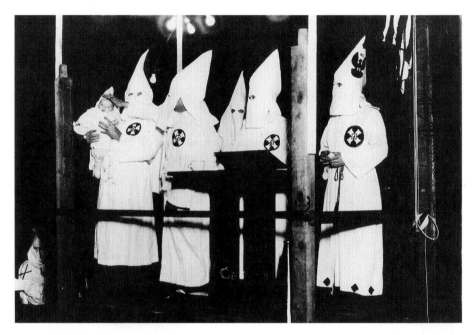

White racist groups such as the Ku Klux Klan terrorized and murdered African Americans. KKK members hid their identities behind white robes and hoods.

believed that blacks were not smart enough and talented enough to compete with their white peers.

Marshall helped prove that this was not true. One such instance was a 1941 case tried in Oklahoma in which an African-American man, W. D. Lyons, was accused of murder. Marshall reported that some people who worked in the court said it was "their first experience in seeing a Negro lawyer try a case."[7] Marshall also noted that NAACP involvement boosted the morale of African Americans. White police officers resented being cross-examined by a black lawyer. Marshall wrote in a report:

> *They all became angry at the idea of a Negro pushing them into tight corners and making their lies so obvious. Boy, did I like that—and did the Negroes in the Court-room like it. You can't imagine what it means to those people down there who have been pushed around for years to know that there is an organization that will help them.*[8]

If a legal case in Alabama needed NAACP support, Marshall caught a train or drove to Alabama. If another case called for his presence in Texas, he went there. Because the NAACP was usually short on money, Marshall often found himself lacking sleep and regular meals. Many hotels were for whites only, so Marshall often stayed in run-down hotels or the homes of local residents. When traveling through the South by rail or bus, he was restricted to segregated seating.

Worst of all, Marshall often faced intimidation and danger. He was considered a troublemaker by many whites, viewed as an outsider from the North who was trying to upset the local order of things. Marshall was frequently the target of hateful remarks and threats. Sometimes he lay awake at night, worried that a mob would capture and hang him.[9]

On one trip to Mississippi, Marshall visited segregated schools to document the poor condition of the buildings and the lack of textbooks. As he drove around the state, his car was accompanied by a hearse filled with armed bodyguards provided for his protection by the state's NAACP chapter.[10]

During the early 1940s, the NAACP's legal activities were curtailed while the nation focused on World War II. But racial problems continued. In 1943, white factory workers went on strike in Detroit after several black workers received job promotions. The strike did not last long, but hard feelings remained. Fights broke out and grew into a full-scale riot. Over a two-day period, thirty-four people were killed, twenty-five of them African Americans, and hundreds more were injured.[11]

Later that summer there was another riot, which affected Marshall more directly because it took place in Harlem. He and two other NAACP leaders rode around in a car and used a loudspeaker to urge citizens to "cool it."[12] Their actions helped calm the situation.

Despite such problems, Marshall kept going with his legal work. When he lost a court case, he did not let the setback depress him. Instead, he used it as a learning experience.

In a Texas case in 1941, Marshall and a lawyer named W. J. Durham had filed suit against the Texas Democratic Party for refusing to let African Americans vote in primary elections. It was the fourth such suit in fifteen years, but none of the earlier ones had been successful.[13] The suit was filed on behalf of Sidney Hasgett, a man who wanted to sign up to vote but was turned down. The case was thrown out on a technicality, but Marshall did not give up. Instead, he went on the offensive. He persuaded the Texas NAACP to fund another lawsuit. In speeches around the country, he criticized the Texas situation. He reminded people that in Europe the United States was standing up against Germany's Adolf Hitler, a champion of racism, and that the nation should not allow racist practices to continue at home.[14]

Members of the NAACP actively searched throughout the South for another African American who would be willing to stand up for their cause. When a doctor named Lonnie Smith agreed to fight the voting limitation, Marshall was eager to take on the case. The new case, *Smith* v. *Allwright*, fared better. Although Marshall lost again, he appealed to a higher court. This was a good strategy because when a higher court agrees to consider an appeal, this means that there will be another trial and another chance to win. The U.S. Supreme Court agreed to review *Smith* v. *Allwright*.

In October 1943, Marshall and another accomplished lawyer, William H. Hastie, presented arguments before the Supreme Court. Their efforts attracted a great deal of attention. Marshall was grateful for the publicity and optimistic that the case would be decided in their favor. Then, in April 1944, the decision was announced: The Supreme Court ruled that all-white primary elections violated the Constitution.

Suddenly, Thurgood Marshall was a celebrity. Newspapers across the United States covered the history-making decision. One newspaper, the *Norfolk Journal and Guide*, reported after the court victory that the NAACP should be respected for its work in seeing that the rights of minorities are protected by the Constitution, just as they are for other citizens.[15]

The *Smith* case is not especially well known today. It is not nearly as famous as some other cases in which Marshall played a central role. But at the time it was one of Marshall's greatest successes as a lawyer and a major victory for civil rights. Later in life Marshall is said to have called it the most important case of his career. *Smith* v. *Allwright* helped establish once and for all that every American adult has a right to participate fully in the election process.

A Supreme Court decision has a tremendous impact, far beyond the people involved in the specific case. The Court ruling also influences future cases at all levels of the legal system. Judges and officials in lower courts use Supreme Court rulings as guidelines for their decisions. Similarly, state legislatures and the U.S. Congress often take Supreme Court rulings into consideration when making new laws or revising existing ones.

The *Smith* decision proved to African Americans that their votes counted. It gave them an incentive to take part in the U.S. political system. In 1940,

Marshall's impressive skill and success in the courtroom were making him a celebrity.

only 3 percent of African Americans living in the South were registered to vote. Three years after the *Smith* decision, that figure was 12 percent. By 1950, 20 percent of the South's African Americans were registered to vote.[16]

Despite this success, Marshall still faced problems, especially in southern states. He often had to put up with shabby treatment, and sometimes his life was still in danger. Perhaps most frightening was an event that happened in November 1946. Marshall was driving down a Tennessee road with two other lawyers and a newspaper reporter when suddenly they were stopped by several cars. Several white law enforcement officers pulled Marshall out of his car, told the others to leave, and hinted that a hanging might be in order.

Marshall's comrades refused to leave, and the officers decided to take Marshall to a jail in a nearby town. There they presented him to the law official, saying he had been driving while drunk. But the official smelled Marshall's breath, said that he could detect no alcohol, and dismissed the charge.

Marshall was then taken by the reporter to Nashville, where he caught the train to New York. He was greatly relieved to escape and would never forget the harrowing incident.[17] Once it was reported in the media, it drew nationwide attention. NAACP members across the United States expressed outrage.

In 1946, Marshall was awarded the Spingarn

Medal by the NAACP. This gold medal, named after early NAACP leader Joel Spingarn, is given yearly to recognize outstanding achievement. It was a great honor.

People who knew Marshall at the NAACP said he was a very hard worker. He would often spend sixteen hours a day preparing for a case. For weeks at a time, he would arrive at the office before 8:00 A.M. and might work until midnight.

Marshall was constantly smoking cigarettes and drinking martinis. Sometimes he drank too much alcohol, but as his court dates neared he always cut back. He wanted to be at his best in court.[18]

Marshall liked being the center of attention. He enjoyed ordering unusual meals at restaurants not just because he liked the food but also to make an impression on other people. One of his favorite restaurant meals was fried roast beef bones.[19]

When it came to civil rights, though, Marshall was all business. He might joke with clients or opposing lawyers—and he was famous for telling humorous stories—but there was more to his storytelling than being the life of the party. He used jokes and tales from his past to make important points, talking about the times he had risked physical harm in pursuing his work, for example. A fellow African-American lawyer said, "He told those stories just to remind people of what he had been through and how far we had come."[20]

Throughout the 1940s, Marshall filed numerous lawsuits against racism. Even though the doctrine of separate but equal still held, many other laws and Supreme Court decisions could be cited to help win cases. One of the most important was the Fourteenth Amendment to the U.S. Constitution, designed to protect the civil rights of all U.S. citizens. Marshall knew that every legal victory for civil rights, no matter how small, would help advance his cause.

In addition to dealing with specific cases involving discrimination, Marshall's work also raised public awareness of the NAACP. Each time Marshall won a court case, it attracted coverage in newspapers and other media. Even when verdicts went against Marshall's clients, the publicity those cases garnered still drew attention to the NAACP. As the years passed, the NAACP became increasingly well known as the major civil rights group in the United States.

Still, making progress in civil rights was a complicated matter. Marshall and others ran into all kinds of resistance. As bad as they were, violent acts and threats were not the only strategies used by people who opposed integration. Even more powerful in some ways was the use of existing law to thwart efforts for change. For example, some colleges or school districts continued using the separate-but-equal ruling to avoid integrating their institutions. If ordered by a court to provide equal opportunities for all students, they would set up separate schools or programs for African Americans. But these separate offerings tended to be far from equal in quality.

So Marshall kept plugging away. He usually focused on education or voting rights cases, but he also took on criminal cases. *Patton* v. *Mississippi,* in 1947, dealt with a murder for which a black man, Eddie Patton, was sentenced to death for killing a white man. But the jury that convicted him was all white. Marshall and the NAACP challenged the fairness of an all-white jury. Once the appeal reached the Supreme Court, the conviction was overturned. The case made important progress in limiting racial discrimination in the selection of juries.[21]

Marshall won another important case, *Shelley* v. *Kraemer,* in 1948. This lawsuit was filed by Louis Kraemer of St. Louis, Missouri, who wanted to prevent an African-American family from moving to his street. All the neighbors had signed a contract known as a *racial restrictive covenant*—an agreement not to sell their homes to minorities. But one property owner broke the contract by selling to the Shelley family, who were African American. Kraemer sued to prevent the Shelleys from moving in. The Supreme Court did not outlaw the racial restrictive covenant, but it did rule that enforcing it was unconstitutional. It was a landmark decision in the battle against segregation.

In this and other cases, Marshall showed his skill.

Many people praised his talent for making good, solid legal points. "In the courtroom Marshall was an awesome figure," said Carl Rowan, a journalist who covered the civil rights movement for decades.[22]

At the same time, Marshall did not win all his cases, although he was victorious in twenty-nine out of thirty-three that reached the Supreme Court. Sometimes, despite his best efforts, appeals were lost. One such case involved Samuel Taylor, an African-American teenager from Alabama who was convicted of rape. Marshall contended that Taylor had confessed to the crime only because police had beaten him, but the Supreme Court did not accept this argument. Instead, the judges let the conviction stand.[23]

Lost court cases were as disappointing to Marshall and supporters of the NAACP as they were to the individuals involved. But Marshall managed to rise above each setback. Discrimination had been a problem in the United States for centuries. It would take much more effort to make real progress.

5

AGENT FOR CHANGE

y the 1950s, Marshall was becoming a hero. A national magazine, *The Afro American*, reported that in its poll for 1952 man of the year, Marshall received more votes than anyone except Adlai Stevenson, who had just been named the Democratic nominee for president.[1]

In February 1953, Marshall was the guest of honor at a banquet in Baltimore. More than six hundred people attended, including celebrities such as NAACP executive director Roy Wilkins, baseball great Jackie Robinson, and boxing legend Joe Louis. One after another, speakers at the event praised Marshall for his work in civil rights.[2]

Marshall did not shy away from such praise, and he continued working very hard to earn it. He and others at the NAACP concentrated their efforts on two major areas: education and voting. Marshall knew that a solid education was vital for everyone, yet many African-American children were denied educational opportunities. They lacked proper facilities, up-to-date textbooks, and enough teachers.

The effort to bring racial equality in public education led to the most famous civil rights case of all. It focused on Linda Brown, a young girl who lived in Topeka, Kansas. Although a nearby school, Sumner Elementary, stood only a few blocks from her home, she was not allowed to go there because she was black. Only white students could attend. Instead, she had to go to an all-black school located twenty blocks away. This school was run-down, had fewer teachers, and lacked other basic resources.

On behalf of Linda Brown and her family, the NAACP filed a lawsuit to allow her to attend the all-white school. A panel of federal judges dismissed the case. They based their decision on the fact that such segregation was not illegal; separate and supposedly equal schools were provided for Topeka's white and black students.

It was the same old thing. But Marshall and the

NAACP refused to give up. They filed an appeal with the U.S. Supreme Court. The *Brown* case was combined with similar cases from Washington, D.C., Delaware, Virginia, and South Carolina. The problem was a national one and not an isolated instance. But the case was named after the *Brown* lawsuit, in part to highlight the fact that racial segregation was a problem in places like Kansas, too, and not just in southern states. The full name of the new case was *Oliver L. Brown et al* v. *Board of Education of Topeka, Kansas*. In the years since, it has become known simply as *Brown* v. *Board of Education*.

When the Supreme Court agreed to consider the *Brown* case, Marshall knew it was a great opportunity. Could he convince the Court that separate but equal was not working?

In the weeks leading up to the Supreme Court hearing, Marshall and an NAACP legal team labored to prepare their arguments. They worked day and night, weekdays and weekends. Sometimes the hours were so long that lawyers and staff on the case did not go home at all. They slept at the NAACP's main office and woke up early to start again the next morning. Then they spent a week in Washington, holding mock arguments at Howard University. Professors and students barraged the attorneys with the kinds of tough questions they could expect from the Supreme Court justices. Marshall and the others kept refining the material.[3]

It was a tense time, and Marshall knew what was at stake. He stuck to his convictions in this important issue and in other areas as well. He believed, for example, that it was important for people to respect one another. Just because another lawyer disagreed with him about civil rights or other issues, that did not necessarily make him or her an enemy.

This was the stance Marshall took with John W. Davis, his chief opponent in the *Brown* case. Davis was a distinguished attorney who had been the Democratic nominee for president of the United States in 1924. He had argued more than one hundred cases before the Supreme Court and was a highly skilled lawyer. Marshall greatly admired him. During law school, Marshall had sometimes skipped classes to hear Davis argue cases before the Supreme Court.[4]

Just a few days before the presentation of arguments in the *Brown* case, Marshall and Davis met for lunch. This was a time when many white southerners would have refused to dine with a black man, and some NAACP officials criticized Marshall for associating with someone they considered an enemy. But Marshall responded, "We're both attorneys, we're both civil. It's very important to have a civil relationship with your opponent."[5]

On December 9, 1952, Marshall and Davis were

Marshall, second from left, argued thirty-three cases before the Supreme Court—and he won twenty-nine of them.

ready to present their arguments to the Supreme Court. The case had generated a great deal of publicity, and a large crowd had gathered at the Supreme Court building. After some preliminary presentations, it was Marshall's turn to address the Court. When he rose to speak, he had everyone's attention.

Marshall was a big man. He was six feet two inches tall and for most of his life weighed well over two hundred pounds. Standing to make a speech or present an argument in court, he was a commanding presence. He also had a voice that made people stop and listen.

Never was Marshall's eloquence more crucial than

on this day. But after he had given his carefully prepared remarks and responded to questions from the justices, he was not sure if he had been forceful enough. Next, Davis made his arguments and the day's discussions were ended. Then Marshall could do nothing but wait. This is the usual procedure with the Supreme Court; it takes months to consider the attorneys' arguments before making a decision.

In June 1953, the Supreme Court was expected to announce its ruling in the *Brown* case. But instead, the justices scheduled another session for later that fall. They had some new questions. Then that session was postponed. Marshall and the others finally appeared before the Court in December. For two days Marshall again argued that school segregation violated the Constitution.

On May 17, 1954, the decision in *Brown* v. *Board of Education* was announced by Chief Justice Earl Warren. On this momentous day in the nation's legal history, the justices ruled unanimously in favor of the Brown family and others who had been denied equal educational opportunities.

The Court opinion included several important points. First, the justices made it clear that they had not based their decision on earlier cases, such as the famous *Plessy* v. *Ferguson* case of 1896. Instead, they said, "We must consider public education in the light

Marshall celebrates the Supreme Court's ruling against segregation in schools with fellow lawyers George Hayes, left, and James Nabrit, right.

of its full development and its present place in American life throughout the Nation."[6]

They also stated that segregation in education hurt African-American children. They pointed out that children who are denied educational opportunities cannot be expected to succeed in life. As a result, the Court rendered its decision—agreed to by all nine justices—that "in the field of public education the doctrine of 'separate but equal' has no place. Separate educational facilities are inherently unequal."[7]

The victory was a stunning one. Many consider it the single most important Supreme Court case of the past hundred years. Certainly, it was the greatest legal triumph of the civil rights movement. Perhaps more than any other single event, this ruling opened the door to equality for all American citizens.

The case was also important far beyond the American legal system and the borders of the United States. *Brown* affected the interpretation of law in countries around the world.[8] In nations such as South Africa, the case served as a legal and moral example that helped in the fight there for equal rights for all citizens.

At home, a major effect of the *Brown* case was that it drew attention to some of the other laws in place at that time. For example, most southern states had laws requiring separation of the races in hospitals. There were segregation rulings covering everything from

The law said black students could go to the same schools as whites—but that did not mean they were welcomed. This Little Rock, Arkansas, student was jeered at by an angry crowd.

telephone booths to circuses. In some states, it was against the law for textbooks used by white students to be stored with those used by black students. Laws imposed fines or imprisonment for anyone printing or distributing written material in favor of interracial marriage.[9]

The publicity surrounding *Brown* v. *Board of Education* helped inspire many citizens—black and white—to focus their energy on civil rights. Marshall's fame grew even wider. In March, his portrait appeared on the cover of *Time*, a newsmagazine read by millions.

Years later, looking back on the case, Marshall gave much of the credit to Charles Hamilton Houston. His longtime friend and mentor had died in 1950, just a few years before this far-reaching civil rights decision. Recognizing the role Houston had played, Marshall said, "The school case was really Charlie's victory. He just never got a chance to see it."[10] Marshall was thrilled with the Court ruling, but he was realistic too; it would take time and effort before all the states fully obeyed the decision.

Near the end of 1954, Marshall faced a personal tragedy. He was devastated by the news that Buster had terminal cancer. When Marshall learned that his wife had only weeks to live, he nearly collapsed.[11]

For the final six weeks of Buster's life, Thurgood Marshall devoted himself to caring for her at their apartment in Harlem. On her forty-fourth birthday, February 11, 1955, Vivian Marshall died. Vivian and Thurgood had no children, and his job had often kept them apart during the twenty-five years of their marriage. Still, they had shared many happy memories, and Vivian's death was a shattering loss.

Marshall took a leave of absence from the NAACP to deal with his grief. He traveled to Mexico for a change of scene. When he returned to his job, he began working on the follow-up issues related to school desegregation.[12]

In December 1955, Marshall married Cecilia Suyat, who went by the nickname Cissy. Born in Hawaii, she worked as a secretary at the NAACP's New York head-quarters, where she and Marshall met. Because the marriage took place just eleven months after the death of Marshall's first wife, some people gossiped about the relationship. But the couple's friends pointed out that a six-month period following the death of a spouse was considered a respectable waiting period before remarrying. They also said that Marshall was the type of person who needed to be married.[13]

In late 1955 and early 1956, Marshall and his colleagues at the NAACP became aware of a plan to boycott city buses in Montgomery, Alabama, because they were segregated. As the boycott unfolded, Marshall learned about a young minister who was at the heart of the protest. His name was Martin Luther King, Jr. Marshall later said that he had not previous-ly heard of King, although he had known his father.[14] This was before Martin Luther King, Jr., became famous throughout the United States.

Marshall was not sure how the NAACP should respond to the news of the boycott. He did not agree with all of King's views. King argued for a nonviolent approach to ending segregation, as did Marshall. But King, an admirer of India's leader Mahatma Gandhi, wanted to try strategies Gandhi had used to protest the British rule of India. King believed that nonviolent boycotts and public protests would aid his fight for civil rights. Marshall disagreed, fearing that such actions might backfire. He had seen the terrible results of race riots in several cities and worried that any protest, even nonviolent, could inflame southern whites and lead to violence.[15] Instead, Marshall believed that the best and safest way to win equal rights was through the courts.

It was the height of the civil rights movement, and

Martin Luther King, Jr., preached that nonviolent protest was the pathway to civil rights. Thurgood Marshall believed that change would come through the legal system.

many people disagreed about how to accomplish their goals. Many agreed with Martin Luther King, Jr., that civil disobedience—refusing to obey unfair laws, staging protests, and so forth—was the best approach. But Marshall believed firmly in the judicial system.

In a 1956 speech in Raleigh, North Carolina, Marshall spoke about this issue. It had become obvious that despite the *Brown* decision, there was widespread resistance to carrying out the Supreme Court ruling. He told the large crowd that the NAACP was willing to negotiate with local officials about the details of desegregation—but it would not back down until schools admitted both white and black students. "We shall resort to the courts and ballot when there is no other way to work out integration," he said. "And we shall do this peacefully, lawfully and in the true American tradition."[16]

In August 1956, the Marshalls' first child was born. They named him Thurgood Jr. after his father. Marshall, who had no children from his first marriage, was pleased to become a parent.

Professionally, Marshall was dealing with some of the most powerful people in American society. One of them was J. Edgar Hoover, the director of the Federal Bureau of Investigation (FBI). Hoover had great concerns about the civil rights movement. He was more interested in controlling threats to the nation's stability than in protecting equal rights for all citizens. To Hoover, the biggest threat was Communism.

Marshall was also concerned about the impact the Communist Party had on some African Americans. Some civil rights activists, such as longtime leader W. E. B. Du Bois, believed the Communist philosophy could benefit minorities in the United States; Communism challenged the existing power structure and seemed to promote equal rights for all. But Marshall disagreed with this view of Communism. He thought the Communist Party pretended to support the needs of African Americans while it really cared only about its own goals.

Marshall did what he could to keep Communists out of the NAACP. He let FBI director Hoover know that he wanted all Communists out of the organization. Marshall also obtained FBI information about participation by Communists in civil rights activities so that he could limit any influence they might have and so the NAACP's reputation would not be damaged. Some people criticized Marshall's efforts in reaction to the threat of Communist influences, but he was not apologetic. "I did more than anybody else did and if you don't believe me, ask," he said.[17]

Marshall's concern was based not only on his strong belief in the law; he also believed that the efforts of some civil rights leaders were too radical to be effective. He feared that they would backfire and lead to violence in which African Americans would be hurt or killed.[18]

Another problem was that the civil rights movement lacked support in some key areas. Some political leaders said they were against segregation but did little to fight against it. President Dwight Eisenhower, for example, gained attention by taking action to enforce federal court rulings, but Marshall thought Eisenhower should have spoken out more in support of equal rights.

In July 1958, Cecilia Marshall gave birth to a second child. They named him John. Although Marshall was older than many parents, he relished the prospect of raising two sons.

In 1959, Marshall met Kenyan leader Tom Mboya, who was visiting the United States. Mboya was impressed with Marshall and invited him to come to his country to help in the drafting of a constitution for Kenya as it moved toward independence from Great Britain.

Marshall's arrival in Kenya in January 1960 created controversy; he was there at the invitation of a man who was considered by some people, both in Africa and America, to be a radical leader. As a result, Marshall was banned from the conference where the constitution was being written. When he was not allowed to enter, Marshall asked to speak to a crowd waiting outside. A police officer refused, but Marshall asked if he could offer just "one word of greeting." The policeman agreed that this would be all right.[19]

Marshall stepped forward, quieted the crowd by waving his arms, then shouted, *"Uhuru."* The crowd responded with a huge cry, for the African word had a highly emotional meaning: "Freedom now."[20]

After leaving Africa, Marshall traveled to London, England, where he continued working on behalf of the Kenyans. His efforts stirred up controversy in the United States. Some criticized him for meddling in African affairs. Others praised him for supporting the people who shared the ancestry of African Americans.

While in London, Marshall met Prince Philip and again demonstrated his quick wit. The prince asked jokingly, "Do you care to hear my opinion of lawyers?" Marshall answered with a smile, "Only if you care to hear my opinion of princes."[21]

Upon returning to the United States, Marshall faced the challenges created by a new wave of civil rights protests. A number of cases before the Supreme Court involved sit-ins. In a typical civil rights sit-in, blacks, sometimes accompanied by white supporters, would gather at a place that served white patrons only—a restaurant, for example. They would sit down and refuse to leave, sometimes for days, in defiance of local or state segregation laws. Sit-ins often led to the arrest of the protesters, but they also sparked news coverage of civil rights issues and placed pressure on those trying to maintain segregation.

At first, Marshall disapproved of this tactic. He had always been dedicated to preserving the law and using it as the basis for protecting people's rights. The idea of breaking the law bothered him. The protesters believed their actions were justified, necessary to call attention to the fact that such laws were unfair in the first place.

Eventually, Marshall came to support these non-violent protest strategies. He listened when some of the more activist members of his staff pointed out that the Fourteenth Amendment to the Constitution provided equal protection for all citizens. When people went into a restaurant and were refused service, their constitutional rights were being violated.

After meeting with other civil rights activists, Marshall agreed to provide legal support for the protesters, including setting funds aside for their legal defense. "Once a store is opened to the public it means it is open to everybody—without discrimination," he said.[22]

A 1961 Supreme Court case, *Garner* v. *Louisiana*, involved just such a protest. The original incident took place in Baton Rouge, Louisiana, where some college students were jailed and fined for sitting down in a restaurant and refusing to leave unless they were served. Although the case bothered Marshall at first because his clients had intentionally broken the law, he believed in its purpose of protecting individual rights.[23] Marshall agreed to appeal the conviction with the help of the NAACP. He successfully argued the case before the Supreme Court in December 1961. In a unanimous ruling, the Court overturned the students' conviction.[24]

As it turned out, this was the last NAACP case Marshall would argue in the Supreme Court. At the time Marshall did not know it, but President John F. Kennedy had other plans for him.

6

MOVING TO THE
BENCH

hortly after John F. Kennedy took office as president in 1961, people began to suggest that he appoint Thurgood Marshall to a federal judgeship. Kennedy was a supporter of civil rights, and Marshall was well known for his legal abilities.

For a while, it seemed that Marshall might not accept such an appointment. He believed that during his presidential campaign, Kennedy had taken credit for accomplishments that were actually attained by the NAACP. He also resented that Robert Kennedy, the president's brother (who later became U.S. attorney

Thurgood Marshall with his wife, Cecilia Suyat, and sons Thurgood Jr. and John.

general), had tried to involve himself in some of the NAACP's business.[1] After the election, Marshall criticized President Kennedy for the lack of civil rights bills in the legislation he was working on in the first few months of his presidency.

But Marshall moved past his hard feelings. In 1961, President Kennedy nominated him to be a judge of the Second Circuit Court of Appeals in New York. This was an honor for Marshall. It was also a step forward for African Americans, who had held few judgeships.

Before taking on this role, Marshall had to be confirmed by the United States Senate. This meant he had to appear before a Senate subcommittee to answer questions. Some of the senators challenged Marshall's abilities and cited statements he had supposedly made against white people. But Marshall stood up to the grilling. The full Judiciary Committee, and then the Senate, voted by a wide margin to confirm him.

Marshall did well in his new position. His years as an attorney helped him adapt quickly to the responsibilities of a judge. During his time on the appeals court bench, not one of his decisions was overturned by a higher court.

On November 22, 1963, President Kennedy was assassinated while traveling in Dallas, Texas. On that day, Lyndon Johnson took office as the thirty-sixth president of the United States. A liberal Democrat,

Johnson continued many of the programs begun by the Kennedy administration. This included promoting new civil rights legislation.

Although new laws may be proposed by the president, it is up to Congress whether or not to enact them. Johnson, who had served for many years in Congress, was highly skilled at working with senators and congressmen to get laws passed. The time was ripe for change. Sit-ins, race riots, and a huge civil rights march in Washington, D.C., on August 28, 1963, created a climate in which Johnson and the members of Congress had growing public support for such legislation.

In the summer of 1964, Congress passed the Civil Rights Act, and President Johnson signed it into law. This important law banned discrimination based on race, color, religion, or national origin in public places where the rules of interstate commerce applied. This meant that service in hotels, theaters, restaurants, trains, and buses must be provided to *all* patrons. The Civil Rights Act of 1964 also mandated, among other things, that public school systems desegregate. It set up a Commission on Civil Rights and a Community Relations Service to deal with race relations

The Civil Rights Act was a major step forward. Built on accomplishments such as those made possible by *Brown* v. *Board of Education*, the act was the most sweeping civil rights legislation that had yet been enacted.

In November 1964, Johnson won the presidential election. He would have four more years in office. Working with Congress is only one part of a president's responsibilities. As head of the executive branch of the federal government, the president holds the ultimate authority for enforcing the nation's laws. When people resisted integration, Johnson took steps to see that laws were obeyed.

Another important presidential role is nominating federal judges and members of the United States Supreme Court, as well as appointing key officials of the executive branch of government. President Johnson wanted to use his authority to increase the number of African Americans in high government office.

When President Johnson named Robert C. Weaver as the secretary of the Department of Housing and Urban Development, the appointment made history. Weaver was the first African American to serve as a cabinet officer. Johnson also broke new ground by appointing Hugh Robinson, a major in the U.S. Army, to become one of his military aides. It was the first time an African American had served in that role as well.[2]

In 1965, Archibald Cox resigned as solicitor general of the United States. The solicitor general assists the attorney general of the United States in carrying out his or her duties. Among other tasks, the solicitor general suggests which cases the Supreme Court should hear and represents the U.S. government in arguing cases brought to the Supreme Court. This means that he or she works closely with Supreme Court officials.[3]

In July 1965, President Johnson asked Thurgood Marshall if he would accept a nomination to become solicitor general. Although he did not tell Marshall at the time, Johnson had a special reason for choosing him. He hoped to nominate an African American to the Supreme Court in the near future. In the highly visible post of solicitor general, Marshall would be able to show his abilities. If he did a good job, perhaps he would be chosen for the next appointment to the Supreme Court.[4]

Before Marshall could actually take the position, he had to be confirmed by the Senate. He appeared before the Senate Judiciary Committee, just as he had nearly four years earlier, but this time he faced no opposition. The senators greeted Marshall and took statements from him and from a few other senators. But they did not pose any questions. They made it clear they were satisfied with his nomination. Less than two weeks later, the full Senate confirmed Marshall's appointment.[5]

Marshall enjoyed working as solicitor general. He said later in life that it "was the best job I ever had."[6]

President Lyndon B. Johnson, right, had his eye on Thurgood Marshall as a possible candidate for Supreme Court justice.

As an attorney for the NAACP, Marshall had already argued many cases before the Supreme Court, so he was already comfortable with that role. As solicitor general, he gained even more experience in the nation's highest court.

Attorneys and others who worked with Marshall during this period praised his efforts. He displayed an ability to get along well with people whether they were high-ranking officials or young, inexperienced lawyers.

Here, as in all phases of his life, Marshall demonstrated his distinctive sense of humor. He was always telling jokes, making funny remarks, or using stories about his past to make points about current issues. He also had a talent for coming up with witty responses. When necessary, though, he was tough and decisive.[7]

All in all, Marshall was a very successful solicitor general. He personally argued eighteen cases and won fourteen of them. He solidified his reputation as an extraordinarily skilled advocate. In 1966, a group known as the Conference of Prince Hall Grand Masters of America awarded Marshall its Distinguished Service Award. It chose him because of his outstanding record in representing the needs of African Americans in the courts. At a dinner held in Marshall's honor, a guest speaker was Tom C. Clark, an associate justice of the U.S. Supreme Court. "No man has given himself to the brotherhood of man more than Thurgood Marshall," he said. "We salute him as Mr. Civil Rights."[8] Years later, in 1981, Supreme Court Justice William Brennan summed up the opinion of many others when he described Marshall as "one of the greatest advocates in the history of the Supreme Court."[9]

While Marshall was serving as solicitor general, President Johnson watched for an opportunity to appoint him to the Supreme Court. Johnson's chance came in 1967, when Justice Clark retired, leaving a vacancy on the bench.

Johnson checked with other leaders about the

selection. Ramsey Clark, the acting attorney general, recommended Marshall highly. "I have no doubt that his future contributions will add even more prominence to his already well established place in American history," Clark said.[10]

In a June ceremony held in the White House Rose Garden, President Johnson announced that he was submitting Marshall's name for the Supreme Court.

I believe he earned that appointment, he deserves the appointment. He is best qualified by training and by very valuable service to the country. I believe it is the right thing to do, the right time to do it, the right man and the right place.[11]

Although Johnson did not refer directly to Marshall's race, the reporters covering the announcement knew this was a major event. In the nearly two-hundred-year history of the United States, no African American had ever served on the U.S. Supreme Court.

The Supreme Court stands at the pinnacle of the judicial branch of government. The Court helps balance the power of the executive and legislative branches. It fulfills a single major purpose: to make sure the Constitution of the United States is upheld. This means that instead of getting involved in ordinary civil or criminal trials, the Supreme Court reviews the decisions of lower courts to make sure they have acted properly.

If Congress passes a law that is not consistent with the Constitution, the Supreme Court can rule the law invalid. If a citizen is convicted of a crime, but the Supreme Court finds that the defendant's constitutional rights were not strictly protected during the trial, the Supreme Court will overturn the conviction.

The nomination to serve on the Supreme Court is the honor of a lifetime. But being nominated did not mean Marshall would automatically become a Supreme Court justice. First he would have to be confirmed by the United States Senate, just as he had for his previous federal positions.

The first step was to go through committee hearings lasting several days. The senators asked Marshall plenty of tough questions. The naming of any new Supreme Court justice is a special event, for there are only nine such positions and justices hold them for life. Sometimes years go by without the appointment of a new justice. And the fact that no African American had ever been chosen for this role brought even more public attention to the process.

Whenever the president submits a nomination for the Supreme Court, there is usually some controversy in the Senate. Senators who are not in the same political party as the president tend to challenge the nominations. In Marshall's case, some senators, especially those from the Deep South, did not want an African American to hold such a high position. This

The U.S. Supreme Court had been all white and all male for almost two hundred years. Many people did not want that to change.

had never happened before, and if they had their way, it never would.

Many journalists, attorneys, and members of the general public agreed. They did not want to see an African American, no matter who he was or what beliefs he held, sitting on the highest bench. Marshall was well known for his liberal views. Political conservatives worried that if he became a Supreme Court justice, he would make an impact not just on civil rights but on other social issues.

Even among African Americans, not everyone supported Marshall's nomination. The Student Nonviolent Coordinating Committee was among the groups opposing Marshall. Originally a civil rights organization opposed to violence, it had become more militant in the mid-1960s. The group, led by Stokely Carmichael, considered Marshall too conservative.

Despite such controversy, Marshall knew he was up to the task. Still, he had faced the confirmation process before, and he knew it could be difficult.

It was a stressful time for Marshall when he walked into the hearing room of the U.S. Capitol, sat down at a table, and began to answer questions. Senator Sam Ervin of North Carolina posed some very difficult questions about the Constitution. If Marshall did not answer them well, some senators might decide to vote against his nomination. But Marshall spoke with confidence.[12]

The biggest roadblock came from Strom Thurmond, a senator from South Carolina who strongly opposed racial integration. Thurmond began asking a series of complex questions. They dealt with obscure details about the Constitution that no lawyer or judge would be expected to know offhand. It was obvious that they were designed to make Marshall look incompetent.

Marshall kept calm and simply said, "I don't know." An expert on the Constitution later said, "No one has ever faced quite so vicious an onslaught as Thurgood Marshall, forced to sit through a demeaning constitutional law and history trivia quiz in order to demonstrate his intellectual acumen and gain Senate approval."[13]

Despite the opposition, Marshall did well. He answered with dignity and kept his composure. After some tense days, the Judiciary Committee voted 11 to 5 to recommend that Marshall be confirmed. When the full Senate voted, the results were 69 to 11 in Marshall's favor. Twenty senators had chosen not to participate in the vote. They did not want to reveal their position in the controversy.[14]

Once again, Marshall found himself in the national spotlight. He was the subject of editorials, newspaper articles, and other publicity. A cartoon in the *Washington Daily News* showed President Johnson holding up a judicial robe to Marshall, with the words "First Negro on the Supreme Court" printed on the front. The cartoon's caption read, "Should be a good fit . . . It took us 177 years to make."[15]

Newsweek magazine praised Marshall's humanity, saying, "And that, after all, is a pretty good qualification for a man to claim when judging his fellow men."[16] Another major publication, *U.S. News and World Report*, not only gave a positive profile of Marshall's accomplishments but also predicted that

Thurgood Marshall was the first African American to serve as a justice of the Supreme Court.

his appointment would provide new momentum for liberal causes.[17]

Marshall swore his judicial oath in a private ceremony in the chambers of Justice Hugo Black, who had served on the Court for thirty years. A southerner who had once been a member of the hate group the Ku Klux Klan, Black had mellowed in his views over the years and had grown to respect Marshall.[18]

Then, on October 2, Marshall took a more public oath in a ceremony at the Supreme Court. His wife, Cissy, and other members of Marshall's family looked on with pride. Also attending were President Johnson, Attorney General Ramsey Clark, former justice Tom Clark, and a crowd of people who had come to see history being made.[19]

With the oath, Marshall became the ninety-sixth justice of the United States Supreme Court. Such a ceremony is always a nationally recognized event, but people took even more notice than usual. As the first African-American Supreme Court justice, Marshall would play a new role in serving his country.

7

JUDICIAL LEADER

In the fall of 1968, Marshall and his family bought a house in an all-white neighborhood of Falls Church, Virginia, just outside Washington, D.C. Their status as the first African-American family in the area attracted attention. When reporters questioned Marshall, he refused to discuss it. He told the press, "It's a private matter where I make my home."[1]

Cecilia Marshall turned an unused bedroom into a study for her husband. She lined the walls with photos and other mementos, such as the Spingarn Medal he had received from the NAACP.[2] They settled into their new house, and by the next summer they were entertaining neighbors with backyard barbecues. Marshall liked to cook, and Maryland crabs were one of his specialties. He also enjoyed hosting dinner parties. Guests included famous people such as singers Harry Belafonte and Lena Horne, as well as fellow Supreme Court justice William Brennan.[3]

Marshall was becoming comfortable with his career on the Supreme Court. As always, he maintained a reputation for being friendly and outgoing. He enjoyed meeting people and making friends. He made it clear that he would not let his important position change his basic desire to enjoy life. He once told an interviewer, "I intend to wear life like a very loose garment."[4]

Even at the age of sixty, Marshall was energetic. Sometimes he could be seen running around in his backyard, playing football with his two sons. He joked that this was the only exercise he ever got. Another pastime was going to the track to watch horse racing.

Marshall held one of the highest positions in United States government, but he was still down-to-earth. He often wore white socks with black shoes, even though he knew that was not fashionable. He liked to joke with the young law clerks at the Supreme Court, calling them "knuckleheads."[5] When he was pleased with their work, he would share snacks with them.

He also entertained them with stories about famous people he had known.

"The Justice entertained his clerks for hours by recalling the wide range of people he had come to know throughout his life," recalled a former clerk. "He could talk as easily about his encounters with Duke Ellington (whom he liked and admired) as he could about testy confrontations with General Douglas MacArthur (whom he disliked and considered a racist)."[6]

But he also made it clear who was in charge. When a clerk pushed too hard with an opinion that differed from Marshall's, he would make remarks such as, "I'm the one who was nominated by President Lyndon B. Johnson and confirmed by the Senate of the United States . . . not you."[7]

On the desk in his office, Marshall kept a small plastic block containing the front-page *New York Times* article announcing the *Brown* decision. It included a photo of Marshall and his legal associates on the steps of the Supreme Court building.

In public appearances, Marshall spoke out on topics he considered important. During the late 1960s, he was concerned about growing social unrest. In a May 4, 1969, speech at Dillard University, he criticized the militancy of some civil rights activists He said that throwing rocks and breaking the law was not the way for African Americans to advance their cause.[8]

Marshall was known for his down-to-earth personality and gift for telling jokes and stories. But he was all business when it came to matters of the Court.

In his work on the Court and in public speeches, Marshall emerged as a leading advocate of affirmative action. This plan was designed to make up for years of discrimination in which minorities had been denied equal access to opportunities. Under affirmative action, people from minority groups would be given special consideration to offset, at least in part, some of the discrimination they or their ancestors had experienced.

For example, when African-American students applied to colleges and universities, race would be a factor along with grades, test scores, and student activities. To allow more minority students access to higher education, greater numbers of African Americans and others who might have been turned away in the past would be accepted.

Under affirmative action, similar concepts were applied in the business world. Through affirmative-action hiring policies, more African Americans and other minorities would be hired or would be promoted to higher-level positions.

While much of Marshall's professional life had focused on civil rights, as a Supreme Court justice he dealt with all kinds of cases. Perhaps the most famous was *Roe* v. *Wade*, a case about abortion decided in 1973.

Abortion has long been one of the most controversial public issues in America. In this historic case, a woman challenged a Texas state statute that made abortion illegal. It was against the law in Texas for a woman to obtain an abortion and for a doctor to perform one. The only exception was when the abortion was medically necessary to save the woman's life. Roe's suit contended that this law unfairly restricted her rights.[9]

A federal district court agreed with Roe. It found that the law was vague and that it infringed on a woman's constitutional rights. The state appealed the verdict, and the Supreme Court agreed to hear the case. In one of its most famous decisions, the Court ruled that preventing women from having abortions was unconstitutional. The vote was a solid majority of 7 to 2. Marshall voted with the majority.

Marshall also helped rule in a number of other important Supreme Court cases. These involved the death penalty, women's rights, reverse discrimination, and other issues.

In a 1972 case, *Furman* v. *Georgia*, the Court considered the legality of the death penalty, or capital punishment. By a 5 to 4 vote, the Court ruled that the death penalty violated the Constitution, at least in the way the states dealt with it at that time. Most justices believed, though, that if properly handled, capital punishment could be allowable under the Constitution. Only Justices Brennan and Marshall disagreed. Marshall believed that it violated the Eighth Amendment, which forbids "cruel and unusual

Thurgood Marshall, back row, second from left, and these other Supreme Court justices ruled in *Roe* v. *Wade*, the controversial case about a woman's right to an abortion.

punishment." He wrote, "Even if capital punishment is not excessive, it nonetheless violates the Eighth Amendment because it is morally unacceptable to the people of the United States at this time in their history."[10]

This statement typified Marshall's beliefs. Some people were more concerned about protecting society from criminals or providing the ultimate punishment; Marshall was equally concerned with the rights of individual citizens. Even when a citizen was convicted of murder, he believed, it was not morally correct for the government to take that person's life.

Sometimes Marshall wrote dissenting opinions for the Court. One of the dissenting justices always presents the views that disagree with the majority's views. In the case of *United States* v. *Kras*, the Court ruled that people could be required to pay a fee when filing for bankruptcy, even if they had very little money. Marshall wrote an eloquent response in which he disagreed. He pointed out that many lawyers and judges did not realize just how difficult life could be for the poor. He said, "No one who has had close contact with poor people can fail to understand how close to the margin of survival many of them are. . . . It is perfectly proper for judges to disagree about what the Constitution requires. But it is disgraceful for an interpretation of the Constitution to be premised upon unfounded assumptions about how people live."[11] This was typical of Marshall's philosophy. He saw himself as an advocate not just for minorities but for anyone who fell out of the mainstream of society.

As he had done throughout his career, Marshall continued to use humor and anecdotes to help make his points when discussing the business of the Supreme Court. Sometimes fellow justices or other officials complained about his talkative, folksy style. But his stories often had a positive effect.

Justice Sandra Day O'Connor, the first woman to serve on the Supreme Court, said that Marshall's stories helped her understand the depth of the problems of racial discrimination. She said that his anecdotes "imparted not only his legal acumen but also his life experiences, constantly pushing and prodding us to respond not only to the persuasiveness of legal argument but also the power of moral truth."[12]

Marshall's personal style drew comments. Another topic of controversy was his health. For most of his time on the Supreme Court, Marshall faced rumors about his poor health. The truth was that he had not taken very good care of himself when he was young, and as an older person he did have several ailments. While on the Court he was hospitalized a number of times for problems ranging from a minor heart attack to pneumonia. But rumors often portrayed him as being more seriously ill than he really was.

Serious illness or death of a justice is a common way that vacancies on the Supreme Court occur. Marshall's health problems caused talk that he might have to retire or that he might die in office. If either happened, President Richard Nixon, a Republican, would have a chance to nominate someone who was more conservative.

Once, when Marshall was in the hospital, President Nixon asked to see Marshall's medical file. Marshall heard about this and took it to mean that the president hoped he would be so ill that he would need to resign. Marshall grabbed the file and wrote across the cover in large letters, "Not Yet!"[13]

Another important case considered by the Supreme Court during Marshall's tenure was *Regents of the University of California* v. *Allan Bakke*. This famous case, decided in 1978, involved "reverse discrimination." White students thought they were treated unfairly because of their race. It was based on a suit filed by Allan Bakke, who had been denied admission to medical school at the University of California at Davis. He later learned that the school had admitted some minority students with lower grades and test scores than his. He said that he was unjustly rejected to give preference to these minority applicants.

The case was complex, and when it reached the Supreme Court, the justices disagreed on how to regard it. Some said that having special advantages for minority students violated the concept of equal rights for all citizens. Others, including Marshall, believed that special efforts were needed to help make up for years of past discrimination. The case was complicated by technicalities involved in interpreting the Fourteenth Amendment, the Civil Rights Act of 1964, and other factors.

After much internal debate, the Court handed down its ruling. It was a compromise: The medical school's decision to deny Bakke's admittance was overturned. This was seen as a victory for those opposed to affirmative action. At the same time, the Court said that colleges could use race as one of the factors in selecting students. So in that sense, the decision supported affirmative action.

Although he was proud of the civil rights progress that had been made, Marshall remained bitter about segregation. He made this clear when the University of Maryland Law School built a new library and named it after him. Marshall refused to attend the dedication ceremony. He said the law school was only "trying to salve its conscience for excluding the Negroes."[14] Even though Marshall chose not to attend, his friend and colleague William Brennan spoke at the dedication. Referring to Marshall, he said, "Perhaps no advocate of our time has more profoundly altered the course of our national development."[15]

During celebrations of the two hundredth anniversary of the U.S. Constitution, Marshall criticized some aspects of the nation's remembrance. He noted that modern Americans should realize that the authors of the Constitution made a serious mistake when they allowed slavery to continue. In a speech in Hawaii, he said that the men who wrote and approved the Constitution created a document that was "defective from the start, requiring several amendments, a civil war and momentous social transformation before human rights were broadly acknowledged."[16]

Marshall may be best known for his stance on civil rights, but he was also extremely interested in other important issues. Sometimes he used his position to speak out on public issues outside the confines of the Supreme Court. In 1985, in a speech at a judicial conference, he talked about the unfair way that capital punishment was administered. He called the death penalty "an unfair element of our criminal justice system," adding that he had "thought and agonized a great deal during my career" over this issue. He argued for several changes.[17]

Marshall said that defendants in death-penalty cases needed better legal protection at the trial stage and during the review process if convicted. He also said: "I do not mean to suggest that these changes would solve the problems inherent in the death penalty. I continue to oppose that sentence under all circumstances." But as long as the death penalty existed, he concluded, everything possible should be done to see that people accused of capital crimes were given the same opportunities as other defendants.[18]

Marshall also had strong views about gender equality. He believed that progress was needed to assure that women had the same rights as men. In his tenure on the Supreme Court, Marshall voted in several women's rights cases, consistently siding in favor of equality. Time and time again, Marshall championed the rights of the individual. One of his enduring traits as a judge was his deep belief that the rights of every person should be protected as fully as possible.

8

VOICE OF WISDOM

As the years passed, Marshall was growing frustrated with his role in the Supreme Court. It is true that Supreme Court justices are free to render opinions based on their own interpretations of the U.S. Constitution. But in fact the justices tend to cluster together around liberal or conservative viewpoints.

Justices Marshall and Brennan were usually at the liberal end of the spectrum. They supported not only civil rights but other issues focusing on individual liberty and the government's responsibility for assuring it. The more conservative justices, such as William

Rehnquist, tended to favor a more limited role for the federal government in the lives of its citizens.

In different eras throughout U.S. history, liberal justices have dominated the Supreme Court at some times, and conservatives at other times. This is because presidents nominate new justices whose views are in line with their own. Just as President Lyndon Johnson, a liberal, had chosen Thurgood Marshall for his liberal views, conservative president Ronald Reagan nominated more conservative justices.

More and more often, Marshall found himself outvoted in Supreme Court decision-making. For most of his time on the bench, the presidents were Republicans with more conservative views than Lyndon Johnson. After Johnson left office in January 1969, he was followed by Richard Nixon, Gerald Ford, Jimmy Carter, Ronald Reagan, and George H. W. Bush. Only Carter was a liberal, and he lost his bid for reelection in 1980. So during those years when vacancies occurred on the Supreme Court, the presidents' appointees were fairly conservative.

Gradually, the numbers shifted. In many cases, votes would be close, 5 to 4 or 6 to 3, and Marshall often found himself on the losing side. He was upset that the rights of individual citizens, in his opinion, were not being sufficiently protected.

In the summer of 1990, William Brennan retired from the Supreme Court. This was a blow to Marshall.

Besides being friends, he and Brennan had often stood together on key issues. Without Brennan, Marshall felt more isolated than before. It bothered him even more that his opinions so often fell in the Court's dissenting viewpoint. More often than not, Supreme Court decisions ran counter to his own views.

At the same time, Marshall found himself lacking the energy for which he had been famous in his earlier years. His health in general was not good. His heart had been damaged by a heart attack years before. He also suffered from problems with circulation in his legs, shortness of breath, and poor vision.[1]

He wanted to stay on the Supreme Court as long as possible. But he realized that he was getting old. At last, he decided that his time as a jurist had passed. On June 27, 1991, Thurgood Marshall quietly retired from the U.S. Supreme Court. His wife, Cissy, and sons, Thurgood Jr. and John, were present in the courtroom for Marshall's last day. Most of the people in the courtroom did not know that Marshall was stepping down from the bench. Only a few close friends, such as William Brennan, were aware that Marshall was ending his twenty-four-year term.

A few days later, Marshall held a news conference. When reporters asked why he had decided to retire, he said, "What's wrong with me? I'm old. I'm getting old and coming apart!"[2] When asked how he would like to be remembered, Marshall's response typified both his

As more conservative justices were appointed to the bench, Marshall found himself outvoted on many Supreme Court decisions.

bluntness and his modesty: "He did the best with what he had."[3]

In some ways, Marshall felt bitter about his last few years on the Court. He was upset that conservatives were dominating the Court. He knew that retiring at this time would give Republican president George H. W. Bush the chance to appoint yet another conservative justice. Still, Marshall felt it was time to end his long and illustrious career.

On January 24, 1993, less than two years after he retired from the Supreme Court, Thurgood Marshall died. He was eighty-four years old. Marshall's death attracted attention throughout the nation and around the world. Television, newspaper, and magazine reporters focused on one of the most important achievements of his life: that he was the first African American in history to serve on the Supreme Court. Many also cited his role in the groundbreaking case *Brown* v. *Board of Education*.

The display of respect and admiration for Marshall was impressive. His body lay in state in the Great Hall of the Supreme Court, covered with an American flag and resting on the same bier that had supported Abraham Lincoln's body in 1865. Between 10:00 A.M. and 10:00 P.M., nearly twenty thousand mourners filed by.[4]

A portrait of Marshall was displayed beside the casket. During the day, someone placed under it a copy of the Supreme Court's written opinion in *Brown* v. *Board of Education*. Across the document, the person had written, "You shall always be remembered."[5]

Several distinguished people spoke at the funeral, including Chief Justice William Rehnquist and former transportation secretary William Coleman. Vernon Jordan, an adviser to President Bill Clinton and former director of the National Urban League, said, "Your voice is stilled but your message lives on. You have altered America irrevocably and forever. Farewell, Mr. Civil Rights."[6]

Thurgood Marshall was buried in Arlington National Cemetery near other notable leaders and veterans of the nation's wars. Not many years before, and for much of Marshall's life, such an honor for an African American would have been unthinkable. Following Marshall's death, an editorial in *The Nation* said, "Thurgood Marshall was the greatest lawman of the age. He did it with a lack of pretension and a gift of humor that shaped but never detracted from the seriousness of his concerns."[7]

Marshall left an impressive legacy. As a champion of the civil rights movement, he had used his skills as an attorney to help African Americans make tremendous progress. When he started out as a young attorney, minorities were greatly limited in the right to seek a good education, the ability to vote without unfair restrictions, even the chance to enjoy public

This statue honoring Thurgood Marshall stands proudly outside the State House in Annapolis, Maryland.

facilities and events alongside white Americans. But Thurgood Marshall helped change all that. In addition, he became an important role model. As the first African American to serve on the Supreme Court, Marshall broke a barrier that had stood for nearly two hundred years.

Thanks in great part to Marshall's years of dedicated service, millions of Americans now enjoy basic rights that once were denied to them. The twentieth century saw a number of great people hold national leadership roles. From civil rights attorney to Supreme Court justice, Thurgood Marshall was one of the most dynamic.

CHRONOLOGY

1908—Born in Baltimore, Maryland, on July 2.

1925—Enrolls at Lincoln University.

1929—Marries Vivian Burey.

1930—Graduates from Lincoln University; enters Howard University Law School.

1933—Graduates from law school; becomes a practicing attorney.

1936—Goes to work as assistant special counsel for the NAACP.

1938—Appointed chief legal officer for the NAACP.

1944—Wins case, *Smith* v. *Allwright*.

1946—Wins case, *Morgan* v. *Virginia*; is awarded Spingarn Medal by the NAACP.

1948—Wins case, *Shelley* v. *Kraemer*.

1954—Wins case, *Brown* v. *Board of Education*.

1955—Wife, Vivian, dies; marries Cecilia Suyat.

1956—Son Thurgood Jr. is born.

1958—Son John is born.

1960—Travels to Kenya and England.

1961—Wins *Garner* v. *Louisiana*, the last case he would argue before the Supreme Court on behalf of the NAACP.

1962—Becomes a federal appeals court judge.

1965—Appointed solicitor general of the United States.

1967—Becomes an associate justice of the United States Supreme Court.

1973—Participates in *Roe* v. *Wade* decision.

1978—Participates in *Regents of the University of California* v. *Bakke* case.

1991—Retires from the Supreme Court.

1993—Dies at age eighty-four.

CHAPTER NOTES

Chapter 1. Lawyer for the People

1. Juan Williams, *Thurgood Marshall: American Revolutionary* (New York: Times Books, 1998), p. 146.

2. Roger Goldman with David Gallen, *Thurgood Marshall: Justice for All* (New York: Carroll and Graf, 1992), p. 62.

3. Louis H. Pollak, "The Limitless Horizons of Brown," *Fordham Law Review*, 1992, vol. 61, pp. 19–20.

4. Legal Information Institute, Supreme Court Collection, Morgan v. Virginia <http://supct.law.cornell.edu: 8080/supct/cases/name.htm>, (September 20, 2001).

Chapter 2. Early Days

1. Randall Walton Bland, *Private Pressure on Public Law: The Legal Career of Justice Thurgood Marshall, 1934–1991* (Lanham, Md.: University Press of America, 1993), p. 5.

2. Howard Ball, *A Defiant Life: Thurgood Marshall and the Persistence of Racism in America* (New York: Crown Publishers, 1998), p. 13.

3. Juan Williams, *Thurgood Marshall: American Revolutionary* (New York: Times Books, 1998), p. 24.

4. Ibid., pp. 24–25.

5. Ball, p. 17.

6. Richard Kluger, *Simple Justice: The History of Brown v. Board of Education and Black America's Struggle for Equality* (New York: Vintage Books, 1977), p. 176.

7. Ibid., p. 177.

8. Michael Davis and Hunter Clark, *Thurgood Marshall: Warrior at the Bar, Rebel on the Bench* (Secaucus, N.J.: Carol Publishing Group, 1992), pp. 32–33.

9. Ibid., p. 40.

10. Ball, p. 45.

11. Ibid.

12. Davis and Clark, pp. 40–41.

13. Ball, p.17.

14. Ibid., p. 25.

Chapter 3. College and Beyond

1. Randall Walton Bland, *Private Pressure on Public Law: The Legal Career of Justice Thurgood Marshall, 1934–1991* (Lanham, Md.: University Press of America, 1993), p. 5.

2. Ibid.

3. Juan Williams, *Thurgood Marshall: American Revolutionary* (New York: Times Books, 1998), p. 42.

4. Ibid., p. 43.

5. Roger Goldman with David Gallen, *Thurgood Marshall: Justice for All* (New York: Carroll and Graf, 1992), p. 24.

6. Bland, p. 5.

7. Williams, p. 50.

8. Ibid., pp. 52–53.

9. Ibid., p. 53.

10. Howard Ball, *A Defiant Life: Thurgood Marshall and the Persistence of Racism in America* (New York: Crown Publishers, 1998), p. 30.

11. Mark V. Tushnet, ed., *Thurgood Marshall: His Speeches, Writings, Arguments, Opinions, and Reminiscences* (Chicago: Lawrence Hill Books, 2001), p. 273.

12. Goldman, p. 26.

13. Ibid.

14. Mark V. Tushnet, *Making Civil Rights Law: Thurgood Marshall and the Supreme Court, 1936–1961* (New York: Oxford University Press, 1994), p. 10.

Chapter 4. Civil Rights Advocate

1. Roger Goldman with David Gallen, *Thurgood Marshall: Justice for All* (New York: Carroll and Graf, 1992), p. 31.

2. Juan Williams, *Thurgood Marshall: American Revolutionary* (New York: Times Books, 1998), p. 89.

3. Ibid., pp. 90–91.

4. Howard Ball, *A Defiant Life: Thurgood Marshall and the Persistence of Racism in America* (New York: Crown Publishers, 1998), p. 58.

5. Ibid.

6. Carl T. Rowan, *Dream Makers, Dream Breakers: The World of Justice Thurgood Marshall* (Boston: Little, Brown and Company, 1993), pp. 112–113.

7. Mark V. Tushnet, *Making Civil Rights Law: Thurgood Marshall and the Supreme Court 1936–1961* (New York: Oxford University Press, 1994), p. 62.

8. Ibid.

9. Ball, p. 69.

10. Adam Cohen, "Thurgood Marshall: The Brain of the Civil Rights Movement," *Time*, June 14, 1999, p. 172.

11. Ball, p. 89.

12. Ibid.

13. Williams, p. 109.

14. Ibid., p. 110.

15. Ibid., pp. 111–112.

16. Ball, p. 78.

17. Ibid., p. 70.

18. Williams, p. 212.

19. Ibid.

20. Martin Weil and Stephanie Griffith, "Marshall Transformed Nation in the Courts," in *Thurgood Marshall: Associate Justice of the Supreme Court: Memorial Tributes in the Congress of the United States* (Washington, D.C.: U.S. Government Printing Office, 1994), p. 176.

21. Ibid., p. 266.

22. Jill Rachlin, "The Kick in Marshall's Beef Stew," *People Weekly*, February 22, 1993, p. 16.

23. Goldman, p. 67.

Chapter 5. Agent for Change

1. Juan Williams, *Thurgood Marshall: American Revolutionary* (New York: Times Books, 1998), p. 218.

2. Ibid.

3. Ibid., p. 213.

4. Michael Davis and Hunter Clark, *Thurgood Marshall: Warrior at the Bar, Rebel on the Bench* (Secaucus, N.J.: Carol Publishing Group, 1992), p. 152.

5. Williams, p. 215.

6. Howard Ball, *A Defiant Life: Thurgood Marshall and the Persistence of Racism in America* (New York: Crown Publishers, 1998), p. 132.

7. Ibid., p. 133.

8. Louis H. Pollak, "The Limitless Horizons of Brown," *Fordham Law Review*, 1992, vol. 61, p. 21.

9. Carl T. Rowan, *Dream Makers, Dream Breakers: The World of Justice Thurgood Marshall* (Boston: Little, Brown and Company, 1993), p. 185.

10. Ball, p. 46.

11. Davis and Clark, p. 180.

12. Williams, p. 236.

13. Davis and Clark, p. 181.

14. Williams, p. 245.

15. Ibid., p. 247.

16. Davis and Clark, p. 183.

17. Williams, p. 257.

18. Juan Williams, "The Strangest of Bedfellows," *Newsweek*, September 14, 1998, p. 33.

19. Williams, *Thurgood Marshall: American Revolutionary*, p. 285.

20. Ibid.

21. Ibid., p. 286.

22. Ibid., p. 287.

23. Ball, p. 174.

24. Ibid.

Chapter 6. Moving to the Bench

1. Juan Williams, *Thurgood Marshall: American Revolutionary* (New York: Times Books, 1998), pp. 291–292.

2. Michael Davis and Hunter Clark, *Thurgood Marshall: Warrior at the Bar, Rebel on the Bench* (Secaucus, N.J.: Carol Publishing Group, 1992), p. 263.

3. Ibid., pp. 245–246.

4. Randall Walton Bland, *Private Pressure on Public Law: The Legal Career of Justice Thurgood Marshall, 1934–1991* (Lanham, Md.: University Press of America, 1993), p. 129.

5. Howard Ball, *A Defiant Life: Thurgood Marshall and the Persistence of Racism in America* (New York: Crown Publishers, 1998), p. 190.

6. Ibid.

7. Williams, pp. 319–320.

8. William Brennan, "Justice Thurgood Marshall: Advocate for Human Need in American Jurisprudence," *Maryland Law Review*, 1981, vol. 40, pp. 395–396.

9. Davis and Clark, p. 264.

10. Ibid.

11. Ibid., p. 266.

12. Ball, pp. 195–196.

13. Ibid., p. 197.

14. Williams, p. 337.

15. Ibid., p. 236.

16. "Mr. Justice Marshall," *Newsweek*, June 26, 1967, p. 36.

17. "With Mr. Marshall on the Supreme Court," *U.S. News and World Report*, June 26, 1967, p. 12.

18. Williams, p. 338.

19. Ibid.

Chapter 7. Judicial Leader

1. Michael Davis and Hunter Clark, *Thurgood Marshall: Warrior at the Bar, Rebel on the Bench* (Secaucus, N.J.: Carol Publishing Group, 1992), p. 292.

2. Ibid.

3. Ibid., p. 293.

□□

4. Richard Kluger, *Simple Justice: The History of Brown v. Board of Education and Black America's Struggle for Equality* (New York: Vintage Books, 1977), p. 760.

5. Randall Kennedy, "Fanfare for an Uncommon Man," *Time*, February 8, 1993, p. 32.

6. Ibid.

7. Ibid.

8. Davis and Clark, pp. 288–289.

9. Legal Information Institute, *Roe* v. *Wade*, <http://supct.law.cornell.edu/supct/cases/name.htm>, (October 8, 2001).

10. Howard Ball, *A Defiant Life: Thurgood Marshall and the Persistence of Racism in America* (New York: Crown Publishers, 1998), p. 397.

11. William Brennan, "Justice Thurgood Marshall: Advocate for Human Need in American Jurisprudence," *Maryland Law Review*, 1981, vol. 40, p. 397.

12. Ball, p. 204.

13. Ibid., p. 203.

14. Adam Cohen, "Thurgood Marshall: The Brain of the Civil Rights Movement," *Time*, June 14, 1999, p. 172.

15. Brennan, p. 390.

16. Ted Gesi, "Justice Marshall's Minority Report," *U.S. News and World Report*, May 18, 1987, p. 12.

17. Thurgood Marshall, "Remarks on the Death Penalty Made at the Judicial Conference of the Second Circuit," *Columbia Law Review*, January, 1986, vol. 86, p. 1.

18. Ibid., p. 8.

Chapter 8. Voice of Wisdom

1. Howard Ball, *A Defiant Life: Thurgood Marshall and the Persistence of Racism in America* (New York: Crown Publishers, 1998), pp. 377–378.

2. Ibid., p. 379.

3. Lisa C. Jones, "The Best I Could With What I Had: The Legacy of Thurgood Marshall, 1908–1993," *Ebony*, March 1993, p. 130.

4. Randall Kennedy, "Fanfare for an Uncommon Man," *Time*, February 8, 1993, p. 32.

5. Ibid.

6. "Thousands Gather in Washington, D.C., to Mourn Death of Thurgood Marshall," *Jet*, February 15, 1993, p. 10.

7. Michael Meltsner, "The Late Justice," *The Nation*, February 15, 1993, p. 184.

FURTHER READING

Aldred, Lisa. *Thurgood Marshall*. New York: Chelsea House, 1990.

Branch, Taylor. *Parting the Waters: America in the King Years, 1954–1963*. New York: Simon and Schuster, 1988.

Fenderson, Louis. *Thurgood Marshall: Fighter for Justice*. New York: McGraw-Hill, 1969.

Goldman, Roger, and David Gallen. *Thurgood Marshall: Justice for All*. New York: Carroll and Graf, 1992.

Kluger, Richard. *Simple Justice: The History of Brown v. Board of Education and Black America's Struggle for Equality*. New York: Vintage Books, 1977.

Rowan, Carl T. *Dream Makers, Dream Breakers: The World of Justice Thurgood Marshall*. Boston: Little, Brown and Company, 1993.

Whitelaw, Nancy. *Mr. Civil Rights: The Story of Thurgood Marshall*. Greensboro, N.C.: Morgan Reynolds, Inc., 1995.

Williams, Juan. *Thurgood Marshall: American Revolutionary*. New York: Times Books, 1998.

INTERNET ADDRESSES

A biography and links from the Library of Congress
<http://memory.loc.gov/ammem/today/oct02.html>

Extensive bibliography of sources about Thurgood Marshall, listing books, government documents, magazine and newspaper articles, and more
<http://www.founders.howard.edu/moorland-spingarn/MARSHALL.HTM>

"Freedom of Information Act: Thurgood Marshall"
Government records related to Marshall
<http://foia.fbi.gov/marshall.htm>

INDEX

Page numbers for photographs are in **boldface** type.